Biggest
BLUNDERS
in Sports

by

Paul Hoblin

Published by ABDO Publishing Company, PO Box 398166, Minneapolis, MN 55439. Copyright © 2014 by Abdo Consulting Group, Inc. International copyrights reserved in all countries. No part of this book may be reproduced in any form without written permission from the publisher. SportsZone™ is a trademark and logo of ABDO Publishing Company.

Printed in the United States of America,
North Mankato, Minnesota
052013
092013

 THIS BOOK CONTAINS AT LEAST 10% RECYCLED MATERIALS.

Editor: Chrös McDougall
Series Designer: Craig Hinton

Photo Credits: Chris O'Meara/AP Images, cover, 1; NFL Photos/AP Images, 5, 27, 29; Tony Gutierrez/AP Images, 7; Rick Rycroft/AP Images, 9; Lauren McFalls/AP Images, 11; Lenny Ignelzi/AP Images, 13; Douglas C. Pizac/AP Images, 15; Scott Boehm/AP Images, 17; Lefteris Pitarakis/AP Images, 21; Paul Spinelli/AP Images, 23; Clive Brunskill/Getty Images, 25; Ronald C. Modra/Sports Imagery/Getty Images, 31; Rusty Kennedy/AP Images, 33; David Stluka/AP Images, 35; Michael Probst/AP Images, 37; Winslow Townson/AP Images, 39; Susan Ragan/AP Images, 41; Fort Worth Star-Telegram/AP Images, 43; Chris Carlson/AP Images, 45; Paul Sancya/AP Images, 47; David Cannon/Getty Images, 49; AP Images, 53, 55, 59; Ron Kuntz/AP Images, 57

Library of Congress Control Number: 2013932582

Cataloging-in-Publication Data
Hoblin, Paul.
 Biggest blunders in sports / Paul Hoblin.
  p. cm. -- (Sports' biggest moments)
 ISBN 978-1-61783-921-4
 Includes bibliographical references and index.
 1. Sports--Juvenile literature. 2. Sports--Miscellanea--Juvenile literature. I. Title.
 796.09--dc23
                                                              2013932582

TABLE OF CONTENTS

Chapter 1

BRAIN SLIP BLUNDERS

Defensive end Jim Marshall was one of the most feared players in the National Football League (NFL). He was both tough and athletic. In 19 years, he started what was then a record 282 consecutive games. Most of those games were with the Minnesota Vikings. During Marshall's career, the Vikings' defense was so dominant that it became known as the "Purple People Eaters."

On October 25, 1964, Marshall was having an especially good game on the road against the San Francisco 49ers. Earlier in the contest he had forced 49ers quarterback George Mira to fumble the ball. Marshall's teammate, Carl Eller, picked up the fumble and ran it into the end zone. The touchdown gave the Vikings a 27–17 lead.

That was still the score in the fourth quarter when another 49er, Billy Kilmer, fumbled the ball. Marshall didn't cause this fumble, but he was

Jim Marshall was a member of the Minnesota Vikings "Purple People Eaters" defensive line in the 1960s and 1970s.

right there to recover it. He picked up the football and took off running. He ran and ran, the end zone getting bigger with each step. Out of the corner of his eye, he saw his teammates on the sideline waving at him. Marshall assumed they were cheering him on. By the time he crossed the goal line, he had run 66 yards. He threw the ball high in the air in celebration.

Oddly, the 49ers fans were celebrating as well. That's when Marshall realized that his teammates hadn't been waving to cheer him on; they'd been waving at him to turn around.

"Jim," his out-of-breath teammate yelled, "you went the wrong way!"

He was right. Marshall had run into the wrong end zone. It was a safety. That meant the 49ers were given two points. Luckily for Marshall, his team still won the game.

Dallas Stars forward Patrik Stefan, *right*, battles for the puck in a game against the Detroit Red Wings in 2007.

Stefan's Slip

Anyone who likes sports has daydreamed about breaking away from the pack and running to glory. All eyes are on the track athlete as he sprints to the finish line first. Or on the hockey player as she skates to an open net. Or on the basketball player as he dribbles in for a dunk.

Usually, this moment leads to the athlete being a hero. But not always. Sometimes athletes find themselves alone but still fall flat on their faces.

On January 4, 2007, the Dallas Stars were less than two minutes away from beating the Edmonton Oilers 5–4 in a National Hockey League (NHL)

ANOTHER RACE, ANOTHER CRASH

In the early 1990s, Canadian racecar driver Paul Tracy was an up-and-coming star. During a race in Phoenix in 1993, he lapped every other driver—twice. The only way he could fail to win the race was by crashing, which is exactly what he did. While trying to lap a driver for the third time, Tracy spun off the track and ended up against a wall. He was okay, but he couldn't finish the race.

game. In a final, desperate attempt to tie the game, the Oilers pulled their goalie and put in an extra player. This move rarely works, and it did not look like it was going to work this time, either.

Stars player Patrik Stefan stole a pass and found himself all alone as he skated toward the Oilers' empty net. All he had to do was nudge the puck into the net to seal the win for his team.

But he didn't do that. Instead, he bobbled the puck and slipped past the net. While he lay on the ice, the Oilers retrieved the puck and raced the opposite way. They scored a game-tying goal with only seconds to go.

"We were bestowed upon a miracle at the end," Oilers coach Craig MacTavish said. "I have never seen anything like it. It's one of those moments in hockey that you'll remember forever. It turned a disaster into a debacle."

Unfortunately for the Oilers, Dallas got the last laugh. The Stars won 6–5 after a shootout.

Racecar driver Paul Tracy experienced some growing pains in his 1993 race in Phoenix.

Lauren's Layup

Lauren Jackson of the Seattle Storm is one of the best basketball players in Women's National Basketball Association (WNBA) history. But even great players make mistakes. On June 18, 2002, Jackson made one of the biggest mistakes of her career.

With her team trailing the Los Angeles Sparks 55–52 in the third quarter, Jackson rebounded a missed free throw and made an uncontested layup. It seemed like a good play, except for one problem:

9

the free throw shooter didn't play for the Storm. She played for the Sparks. That meant Jackson had just scored on her own basket.

The Sparks went on to win by 12, so the extra two points didn't factor into the outcome of the game. If they had only won by two, Jackson's mistake would have been even more embarrassing.

The Seattle Storm's Lauren Jackson looks to shoot during a 2002 WNBA game.

Chapter 2

CELEBRATION BLUNDERS

O ften, when players make a great play, they celebrate. Sometimes, these celebrations lead to disaster.

In a 2001 NFL game, Arizona Cardinals kicker Bill Gramatica made a field goal against the New York Giants. It was only the first quarter, but Gramatica celebrated as though he had just won the game. He jumped into the air and pumped his fist.

If the jump was awkward, the landing was worse. Grabbing his knee, he fell to the ground in pain. Gramatica had torn his anterior cruciate ligament, or ACL. The knee injury was bad enough that he missed the rest of the season.

Arizona Cardinals kicker Bill Gramatica, shown in 2001, was known for his big field goal celebrations.

Lett Me Score, Okay?

Leon Lett was an All-Pro defensive lineman for the Dallas Cowboys. But he is also famous for making some of the biggest blunders in sports history. One of them happened during Super Bowl XXVII after the 1992 season.

In the fourth quarter, a Buffalo Bills player fumbled the football. Lett picked the ball up and ran for the end zone. Everyone, including Lett, thought he was going to score a touchdown. Lett was so sure, he slowed down and waved the ball in celebration.

What he didn't realize was that Don Beebe, a Bills receiver, was chasing him. Just before Lett scored, Beebe knocked the ball out of his hand. It rolled through the end zone for a touchback. The blunder proved to be not too costly, though. Dallas still won 52–17.

OUCH DOWN!?

Bill Gramatica isn't the only football player to injure himself while celebrating. In 1994, San Francisco 49ers defensive back Deion Sanders once injured his groin while doing his famous high step into the end zone.

Failure to Follow the Rules

Sporting events have rules, and athletes get penalized for breaking them—even if they didn't mean to. At the 2001 swimming world

The Buffalo Bills' Don Beebe, *left*, catches up to Leon Lett before stripping him in Super Bowl XXVII in January 1993.

championships, the Australian women's 4x200-meter relay team swam faster than any other team. When the last member touched the wall, her teammates were ecstatic. They cheerfully jumped into the water to celebrate.

Minutes later, they found out that they had been disqualified. Replays showed that they had jumped into the water before another team had finished the race. The Australian team appealed the disqualification. After all, they really had the fastest time, and their celebration in the pool hadn't affected the outcome. But a court upheld the ruling and the Australians were stripped of their gold medal.

Of course, a swim race isn't much like a golf match—but both sports have rules that can't be broken. In 2000, Swedish golfing great Annika Sorenstam made an amazing, 25-foot chip shot during a match between European and US golfers. Unfortunately, it wasn't her turn to play. The United States was given a choice: it could ignore Sorenstam's mistake, or make her try the shot again. The Americans decided to make her try again, and this time she missed the chip shot.

Broken Record

Philadelphia Eagles wide receiver DeSean Jackson must not have learned from Leon Lett's Super Bowl fumble. In a 2008 game against the Dallas Cowboys, Jackson caught a long pass and raced to the end zone. Jackson

Philadelphia Eagles wide receiver DeSean Jackson tosses the ball behind him just before stepping into the end zone in 2008.

NOT AGAIN...

When DeSean Jackson chucked the ball behind him before he'd crossed the end zone, it seemed like the sort of mistake that someone could only make once. Amazingly, though, it was the second time Jackson had fumbled while celebrating too early. During a high school All-Star game, Jackson had once again run away from the pack. He was all alone and only yards from the goal line. To show off, he leapt into the air, did a flip, and set the ball down . . . on the 1-yard line.

is a lot faster than Lett, so there was no way anyone could catch him. All he had to do was hold on to the ball until he stepped across the goal line.

But he couldn't do that. He was so excited by the touchdown he was about to score that he flung the ball behind him to celebrate. Replays showed that he let go of the ball before entering the end zone.

TV announcer Mike Tirico called it "one of the all-time bonehead plays." Thankfully for Jackson, he was not the only one to make a mistake on the play. A nearby official initially ruled it a touchdown. Had a Cowboys defender grabbed the ball, it would have been a turnover. Instead the touchdown was overturned on a challenge and the Eagles got the ball back on the 1-yard line. Running back Brian Westbrook scored on the next play. Dallas got the last laugh, though, winning 41–37.

Keep Going!

Milkha Singh is a legend in India. People there call him the "Flying Sikh." They know that before he became a legend, he was an orphan. He once spent a month sleeping in a railway station. When he started running, India didn't have any trainers or training facilities. He had to learn about the sport on his own.

That's exactly what he did. At first he didn't even know how far 400 meters was, but within a few years he was running that distance in the Olympic Games. India had gained independence from Great Britain in 1947. But the country had not won a track-and-field Olympic medal since. The Flying Sikh was hoping to change that at the 1960 Olympic Games in Rome, Italy.

Singh got off to a great start. He had a big lead. But that scared him. He thought he might not be able to keep up his pace for the rest of the race. So he slowed down.

This turned out to be a huge mistake. By slowing down, he lost his rhythm and never quite got it back. Singh finished fourth in the race. He was only 0.1 seconds behind the runner who won the bronze medal.

POOR PERVIS PASCO

The Kansas State University men's basketball team had upset the University of Colorado in the 2003 Big 12 Tournament. It was *over*. Or so it seemed. The Wildcats were leading, 76–74. Power forward Pervis Pasco intercepted a long Colorado inbounds pass with 3.3 seconds remaining. All he had to do was stand there or dribble out the clock. But he got excited. He stopped thinking. He ran with the ball toward his teammates in celebration and was called for traveling. And wouldn't you know it? Buffaloes guard James Wright promptly banked in a three-pointer to give his team a 77–76 victory. Pasco had gone from hero to goat in a matter of seconds.

The Flying Sikh went on to win lots of other races and became a national hero. But none of those races were in the Olympic Games.

You Can't Catch Me, Unless . . .

In 2006, US snowboarder Lindsey Jacobellis was attempting to be the first Olympic gold medalist in women's snowboard cross history. As she zoomed down the slope, she looked over her shoulder. No one was within several yards of her. Victory was only seconds away. All she had to do was make it over a couple more jumps and cruise across the finish line.

It seemed simple, even routine—so routine, in fact, that Jacobellis decided to make the most of this moment. When she went off the second-to-last jump, she tucked her legs and grabbed her snowboard and twisted in the air. It was a trick move called a backside method, a way of showing off. When she landed, she lost her balance and fell to the ground. Tanja Frieden of Switzerland charged past Jacobellis and won the Olympic gold medal. Jacobellis settled for second.

Lindsey Jacobellis showboats as she goes off a jump during the 2006 Olympic snowboard cross finals in Turin, Italy.

"I was ahead," Jacobellis said later. "I wanted to share with the crowd my enthusiasm. I messed up."

Chapter 3

WHIFF!

Athletes make mistakes all the time. They trip and stumble; they fumble and bobble. Still, some mistakes are more memorable—and more embarrassing—than others. Just ask former New York Giants punter Sean Landeta.

In January 1986, Landeta trotted onto the field during the first quarter of a playoff game against the Chicago Bears. He caught the snap, dropped the football, and swung at it with his leg.

It was windy that day. Maybe the ball moved before it reached his foot. Or maybe Landeta was afraid of getting the punt blocked, so he kicked too early. For some reason, Landeta's foot never touched the football. Instead, the ball landed on the ground and bounced to Landeta's right. A Bears player picked up the ball and ran it into the end zone.

Sean Landeta played 21 NFL seasons but became known for his 1986 missed punt.

Swing and a Whiff

In 1983, Hale Irwin was one of the best golfers in the world. Earlier in his career, he had won the US Open. And in 1983, he was contending for a British Open championship. On the third day of the four-day tournament, Irwin putted to within an inch or two of the hole. All he had to do was tap the ball into the cup.

To say it was an easy shot is an understatement. The shot was so easy, Irwin didn't bother to take his time setting up. Instead, he casually brushed at the ball with the backside of the putter. Somehow, Irwin missed—not just the putt but the ball itself. The putter bounced off the ground and over the ball.

"I guess I just lifted my head," Irwin said. However it happened, the whiff proved costly. He lost the British Open that year by a single shot.

THIS HAPPENED BEFORE?

Amazingly, Hale Irwin isn't the only player to whiff while putting. All the way back in 1889, golfer Andrew Kirkaldy did the same thing. Like Irwin, he did it while playing the British Open. Also like Irwin, the whiff happened on the 14th hole.

Another Swing, Another Miss

Like punters, tennis players rarely miss the ball completely. Especially great tennis players. Roger Federer definitely qualifies as great—maybe

Roger Federer prepares to hit a forehand against Rafael Nadal during the 2010 Madrid Masters.

even the greatest ever. Federer had won 17 major tennis tournaments, more than any other player, through 2012. Of course, great doesn't mean perfect.

At the 2010 Madrid Masters final, Federer faced match point. He was playing his rival, Rafael Nadal. If Nadal won just one more point, he would win the tournament. Federer served; Nadal returned. Federer took a huge swing, trying to crush the ball. It's a shot that Federer usually makes. But this time he didn't make it. In fact, he never even touched the ball. One of the greatest tennis players of all time had completely whiffed.

Super Bowl, Super Drop

Football players drop passes all the time. Usually, people forget about these drops. When they happen during the Super Bowl, though, people have long memories. Just ask Wes Welker. In February 2012, during the fourth quarter of Super Bowl XLVI, Welker jumped up to catch a pass. It was a catch that the New England Patriots' receiver usually made, but this time he didn't. He came crashing to the ground empty-handed.

It would have been a big play, but at the time it didn't seem like a game-changing play. The Patriots were still leading by two points. As it turned out, the opposing New York Giants came back to win the game. Because Welker's drop happened in the Super Bowl, it was analyzed for weeks after the game had been decided.

Super Bowl drops get even more attention when they happen in the end zone. That's what Dallas Cowboys tight end Jackie Smith discovered during Super Bowl XIII in January 1979. Late in the third quarter, the Cowboys trailed the Pittsburgh Steelers 21–14. Cowboys quarterback

DON'T PUNT IT THAT WAY!

Not many punters miss the ball completely, but there are other ways to botch a punt. Especially when it's windy. In 1913, Indiana University Hoosiers punter Clair Scott had to punt from his own end zone. A 50-mile-per-hour (80 km/h) wind was blasting straight at him. Scott kicked the ball as far as he could before the wind blew it backward. Leo Dick, the University of Iowa Hawkeyes' punt returner, ran after the ball. He caught it while standing in the same end zone as Scott. Touchdown Hawkeyes!

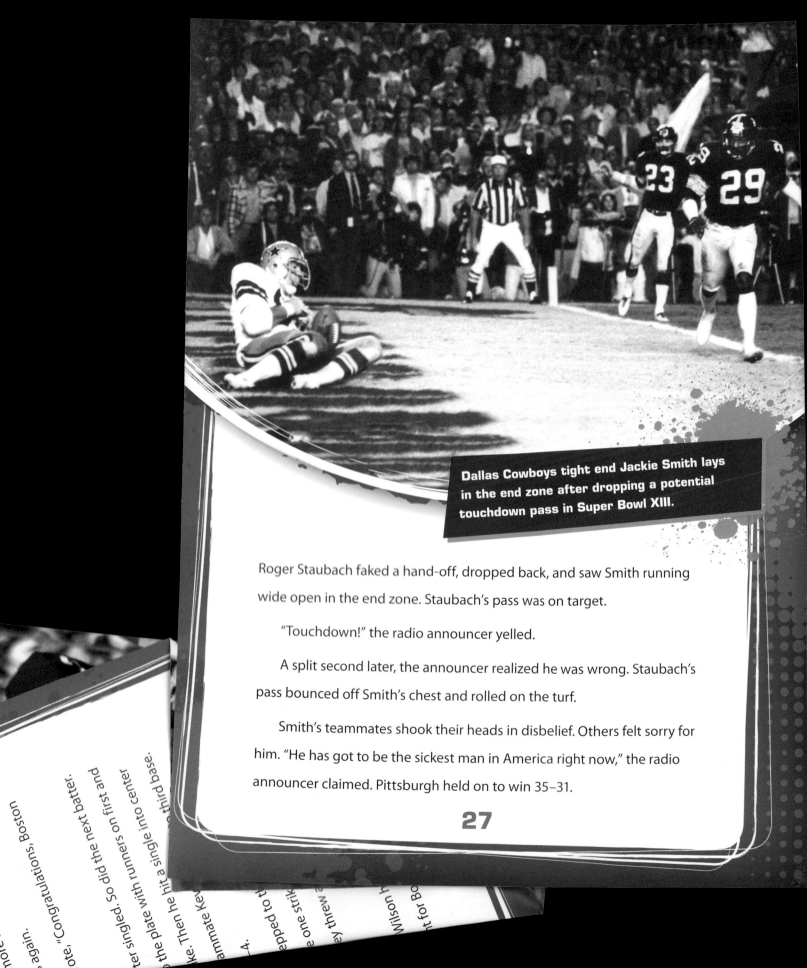

Dallas Cowboys tight end Jackie Smith lays in the end zone after dropping a potential touchdown pass in Super Bowl XIII.

Roger Staubach faked a hand-off, dropped back, and saw Smith running wide open in the end zone. Staubach's pass was on target.

"Touchdown!" the radio announcer yelled.

A split second later, the announcer realized he was wrong. Staubach's pass bounced off Smith's chest and rolled on the turf.

Smith's teammates shook their heads in disbelief. Others felt sorry for him. "He has got to be the sickest man in America right now," the radio announcer claimed. Pittsburgh held on to win 35–31.

"I've Got It" . . . Not

Another bad time to drop the ball is the World Series. New York Giants outfielder Fred Snodgrass knew this from experience. In the final game of the 1912 World Series, Snodgrass's team was beating the Boston Red Sox by a single run in the 10th inning. A Red Sox player hit a fly ball to center field. Snodgrass hardly had to move. The ball fell from the sky, straight into his glove. It was an easy catch.

But Snodgrass didn't catch it. One moment the ball was in his glove; the next it wasn't. The Red Sox went on to tie the game and then to win it.

People remembered Snodgrass's drop for the rest of his life. Even his death didn't make people forget. His obituary read "Fred Snodgrass, 86, Dead; Ball Player Muffed 1912 Fly."

ANOTHER SUPER BOWL DROP

The 1972 Miami Dolphins are the only team in NFL history to go undefeated in the regular season and playoffs. But a blunder by their kicker during the Super Bowl almost cost them their perfect season. When Garo Yepremian's field goal attempt was blocked, he should have fallen on the ball. Instead, he picked up the ball and raised it a[...] throwing, that's what he did nex[...] in the air, and dropped back to h[...] air. It landed in the arms of a Wa[...] in for a touchdown. Luckily for Ye[...] they hadn't, he would likely have [...]

Buckner's D[...]

From 1903 to 1918, the Boston Re[...] one of the greatest dynasties in all of spor[...] that it would take them almost 90 years t[...]

In 1986, it appeared their championsh[...] coming to an end. They held a three-gam[...] seven World Series. During Game 6, the[...] 5–3. It was the 10th inning. There were t[...] Mets batter Gary Carter had a 2–1 coun[...] Sox would finally be World Series cham[...]

The person running the scoreboar[...] Red Sox, World Champions."

Instead of striking out, though, Ca[...] Third baseman Ray Knight stepped t[...] second. He got down to the final st[...] field, scoring Carter and sending t[...]

The Red Sox's lead was down to 5[...] Then Boston pitcher Bob Stan[...] was 3–2. Again the Red Sox we[...] Left fielder Mookie Wilson st[...] game was tied, 5–5.

Then, on the next pitch[...] The ball was headed straig[...]

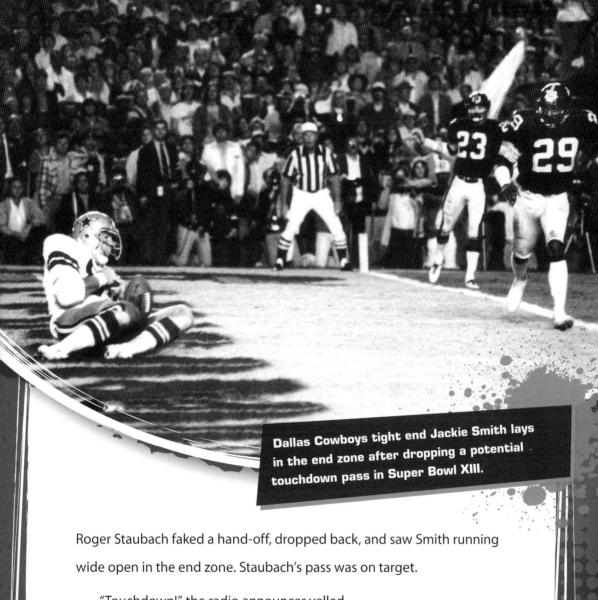

Dallas Cowboys tight end Jackie Smith lays in the end zone after dropping a potential touchdown pass in Super Bowl XIII.

Roger Staubach faked a hand-off, dropped back, and saw Smith running wide open in the end zone. Staubach's pass was on target.

"Touchdown!" the radio announcer yelled.

A split second later, the announcer realized he was wrong. Staubach's pass bounced off Smith's chest and rolled on the turf.

Smith's teammates shook their heads in disbelief. Others felt sorry for him. "He has got to be the sickest man in America right now," the radio announcer claimed. Pittsburgh held on to win 35–31.

"I've Got It" . . . Not

Another bad time to drop the ball is the World Series. New York Giants outfielder Fred Snodgrass knew this from experience. In the final game of the 1912 World Series, Snodgrass's team was beating the Boston Red Sox by a single run in the 10th inning. A Red Sox player hit a fly ball to center field. Snodgrass hardly had to move. The ball fell from the sky, straight into his glove. It was an easy catch.

But Snodgrass didn't catch it. One moment the ball was in his glove; the next it wasn't. The Red Sox went on to tie the game and then to win it.

People remembered Snodgrass's drop for the rest of his life. Even his death didn't make people forget. His obituary read "Fred Snodgrass, 86, Dead; Ball Player Muffed 1912 Fly."

ANOTHER SUPER BOWL DROP

The 1972 Miami Dolphins are the only team in NFL history to go undefeated in the regular season and playoffs. But a blunder by their kicker during the Super Bowl almost cost them their perfect season. When Garo Yepremian's field goal attempt was blocked, he should have fallen on the ball. Instead, he picked up the ball and raised it above his head. If a person can whiff while throwing, that's what he did next. The ball slipped from his hand, went high in the air, and dropped back to him. Then he batted the ball straight up in the air. It landed in the arms of a Washington Redskins player, who then ran it in for a touchdown. Luckily for Yepremian, the Dolphins still won the game. If they hadn't, he would likely have been blamed for the loss.

Miami Dolphins kicker Garo Yepremian scrambles with the ball after a botched field goal attempt in Super Bowl VII.

Buckner's Blooper

From 1903 to 1918, the Boston Red Sox won five World Series. They were one of the greatest dynasties in all of sports. No one could have predicted that it would take them almost 90 years to win another World Series.

In 1986, it appeared their championship drought was at long last coming to an end. They held a three-games-to-two lead in the best-of-seven World Series. During Game 6, the Red Sox led the New York Mets 5–3. It was the 10th inning. There were two outs. The bases were empty. Mets batter Gary Carter had a 2–1 count. Two more strikes and the Red Sox would finally be World Series champions again.

The person running the scoreboard wrote, "Congratulations, Boston Red Sox, World Champions."

Instead of striking out, though, Carter singled. So did the next batter. Third baseman Ray Knight stepped to the plate with runners on first and second. He got down to the final strike. Then he hit a single into center field, scoring Carter and sending teammate Kevin Mitchell to third base. The Red Sox's lead was down to 5–4.

Left fielder Mookie Wilson stepped to the plate next. Soon the count was 3–2. Again the Red Sox were one strike away from a World Series title. Then Boston pitcher Bob Stanley threw a wild pitch. Just like that, the game was tied, 5–5.

Then, on the next pitch, Wilson hit a ground ball to the right side. The ball was headed straight for Boston first baseman Bill Buckner.

Mets left fielder Mookie Wilson runs to first base during Game 1 of the 1986 World Series.

KEEP YOUR EYE ON THE BALL

Baseball has changed over the years, but players still occasionally muff easy catches. Former New York Mets second baseman Luis Castillo won three Gold Gloves for his excellent defense. But many Mets fans only remember him dropping the ball during a 2009 game against their crosstown rival, the New York Yankees. Former Texas Rangers star Josh Hamilton also had a memorable misplay. Going into the last game of the 2012 regular season, the Rangers needed to beat the Oakland Athletics in order to win the division. In the fourth inning, Hamilton ran under what looked like a routine fly ball. But he ran too far. The ball brushed against the end of his glove and then rolled past him. Two runs scored, and the Athletics went on to win the division instead of the Rangers.

All Buckner had to do was field the ball, touch first base, and the Red Sox could try to win the game with their bats.

But Buckner never touched first base—because he never touched the ball. The grounder rolled under his glove and between his legs, and the Mets scored the winning run. They won Game 7 as well, and Boston would have to wait until 2004 to celebrate another World Series victory.

Buckner had an excellent career in the major leagues. He was a good hitter and usually a good fielder. But he will forever be remembered for his error in Game 6 of the 1986 World Series.

Boston Red Sox first baseman Bill Buckner walks off the field after committing his famous error in Game 6 of the 1986 World Series.

Chapter 4

USE YOUR HEAD BLUNDERS

Sports blunders often involve the head. Whether it's failing to duck or failing to think, players' noggins are frequently their downfall.

In 1997, Gus Frerotte was the Washington Redskins' starting quarterback. After scoring a first-half touchdown against the New York Giants, he celebrated by chucking the football against a padded bleacher wall. He then charged the wall and head-butted it.

He spent the rest of the first half wincing in pain. At halftime he was taken to a hospital. He had sprained his neck. He left the hospital in a neck brace. The Giants game was Frerotte's twenty-ninth consecutive start for the Redskins. He started again the next week but never became a consistent starter again. He left Washington in 1999 and bounced around with six different teams through 2008.

Gus Frerotte didn't have much to celebrate with the Washington Redskins after his 1997 head-butt celebration.

Get Out of the Ring, Mom!

In 1989, boxer Tony Wilson fought Steve McCarthy. McCarthy knocked Wilson to the mat. When Wilson looked up, he was surprised to see his mother in the ring.

He was even more surprised to see her holding one of her high heels and hitting McCarthy on the head with it. She hit McCarthy so hard that he had to leave the ring to take care of the bleeding. McCarthy refused to go back in the ring, so the official awarded the victory to Wilson. Still, Wilson banned his mother from attending any more of his fights.

Never Show Your Bare Head

With 10 seconds left in a 2002 NFL game, the Cleveland Browns were beating the Kansas City Chiefs by two points. Dwayne Rudd sacked Kansas City quarterback Trent Green. Or that's what Rudd thought had happened, anyway. Had it happened, it would have ended the game. In his excitement, Rudd ripped off his helmet and threw it in the air.

France's Zinedine Zidane, *left*, is shown a red card after he head-butted Italy's Marco Materazzi in the 2006 World Cup.

What Rudd didn't realize was that Green had pitched the ball to a teammate before getting tackled. It's against the rules for a player to take off his helmet while a play is still going on. So even though the clock had ticked down to zero, the referees gave Kansas City one more play. This time the Chiefs brought in their field goal kicker. He made the kick and Kansas City won the game.

How Many Outs Are There?

In a 2003 Major League Baseball (MLB) game, Boston Red Sox outfielder Trot Nixon caught a fly ball to end the top of the eighth inning. Or so he thought. He tossed the ball into the stands and started jogging to his dugout. One problem—there were actually only two outs.

NOT A GREAT WEEK

In his prime, Jose Canseco was one of the most feared hitters in the major leagues. No one ever accused him of being a great fielder, though. In a 1993 game for the Texas Rangers, Canseco ran after a deep fly ball. As he reached the warning track, he looked down at his feet. The fly ball missed his glove, hit his head, and bounced over the wall for a Cleveland Indians home run.

That wasn't his first or his last sports blunder. Later that week, in fact, he convinced his manager, Kevin Kennedy, to let him pitch, even though the last time he had pitched was in high school. In his one major league inning as a pitcher, Canseco walked three batters and gave up three runs. He also injured his arm badly enough that he needed season-ending surgery.

Outfielder Jose Canseco throws a pitch during a 1993 Texas Rangers blowout loss to the Boston Red Sox.

By the time Nixon realized this, the damage had been done. The Anaheim Angels had two runners on base and one scored. Boston lost the game, 6–2.

"It was a boneheaded play," Nixon said afterward. "It was just stupid."

More Bad Counting

Chris Webber is remembered as a star basketball player in college and in the National Basketball Association (NBA). But he's also remembered for a really bad decision he made during the 1993 college national championship game.

Webber's University of Michigan Wolverines trailed the University of North Carolina Tar Heels 73–71 with time running out. With 19 seconds left, Webber grabbed a rebound and dribbled past half court. Pretty soon opposing defenders were all over him. So Webber, in front of his team's bench, signaled for a timeout. The reason for the timeout made sense. It would give the Wolverines' coach a chance to draw up one final play to tie or win the game.

There was a problem, though. Michigan didn't have any timeouts left to call.

The Wolverines were given a technical foul. North Carolina got the ball back plus two free throws. Donald Williams made both free throws. The Tar Heels then inbounded the ball back to Williams. He was immediately fouled and made both free throws. The Tar Heels won the national championship 79–71.

Up until the timeout signal, Webber had had a great game. He had scored 23 points and snatched 11 rebounds. But knowing that didn't make Webber feel any better. After the game he said that the timeout "probably cost us the game."

What Was He Thinking?

It's not only players who make blunders. Coaches do, too. Former Detroit Lions coach Marty Mornhinweg made one of the all-time worst coaching blunders in 2002.

Michigan's Chris Webber didn't look happy after his accidental "timeout" in the 1993 championship game.

The Lions went to sudden-death overtime in a game against the Chicago Bears. Whichever team scored first would win the game. The Lions won the coin flip. But instead of asking to get the ball first, Mornhinweg decided to kick the ball to the Bears. Later, he explained that he wanted the wind to be at his team's back. But the decision didn't make much sense to Lions fans, especially after the Bears kicked a field goal to win the game.

Lett's Lunge

Leon Lett was a fearsome football player. But he also made two of the biggest blunders in NFL history. The first was against the Buffalo Bills in the Super Bowl. The second happened on Thanksgiving of 1993.

That Thanksgiving Day itself was strange. The game was played in Texas, which is known for its year-round warm weather. On this day, though, it was snowing. In fact, it was the coldest regular-season game ever played in Dallas. Ice froze on players' eyebrows.

With around 15 seconds left to play, the Cowboys led the Miami Dolphins by one point, 14–13. The Dolphins brought out their field goal kicker to attempt a game-winning kick. One of Lett's teammates blocked the kick, and everyone assumed the Cowboys had escaped with the victory. Cameras switched to Cowboys' owner Jerry Jones raising his hands triumphantly.

"Wait a minute. Wait a minute," an announcer said.

The cameras went back to the field, where for some reason Miami was celebrating. After a series of replays, it was discovered that Lett had gone running after the blocked field goal. Lett dove, slid on the snow-covered field, and tried to grab the ball. If he hadn't touched the football, the game would have been over. But by touching the ball, it became a fumble. The wet, icy football slipped out of his hands, and the Dolphins recovered it.

This time they made the field goal. The final score: Dolphins 16, Cowboys 14.

Is Anyone Using His Head?

In 2012, Kent State University played a college football game against Towson University. When a punt by Kent State bounced off a Towson player, Kent State recovered the football. Andre Parker, the player who recovered the ball, took off running—the wrong way. In other words, he ran back in the direction he'd originally come from.

He ran 58 yards. Parker would have run all the way to the wrong end zone if Towson had only let him. But for some reason they didn't. They chased Parker down and tackled him almost 30 yards short of the goal line.

Then the referees realized that they should have called the play dead as soon as Parker recovered the football. They put the ball back

Sven Kramer of the Netherlands, *right*, reacts after learning he was disqualified from the 10,000-meter race at the 2010 Olympics.

on the 7-yard line where Parker first touched it. Kent State was awarded the football.

To sum up: the Kent State player shouldn't have run the wrong way. Towson shouldn't have tackled him. And the referees shouldn't have allowed either of those things to happen. At least it was all sorted out in the end.

Chapter 5

BLAME THE OTHER GUY BLUNDERS

Since most sports blunders happen on the field, it's usually athletes who make them. But not always. Sometimes it's fans or technology or even wildlife that is to blame. Or sometimes it is a game official.

Perfect games don't happen often in baseball. In fact, through 2012 a pitcher had retired all 27 batters in order only 23 times in major league history. So when Detroit Tigers pitcher Armando Galarraga retired the first 26 Cleveland Indians batters on June 2, 2010, people tuned in to watch the final out. What they saw instead was a blown call.

On the third pitch Jason Donald hit a weak ground ball toward first baseman Miguel Cabrera. Galarraga rushed over to cover first base. He got the ball and clearly touched the bag before Donald, but umpire Jim Joyce ruled the runner safe.

Detroit Tigers pitcher Armando Galarraga appears to record the twenty-seventh out as umpire Jim Joyce watches in 2010.

Galarraga retired the next batter to secure the 3–0 win. Joyce quickly admitted he had blown the call. Galarraga had every right to be bitter, but the game became remembered for the sportsmanship the player and umpire showed after. Joyce apologized to Galarraga and they shook hands the next day at home plate.

"I'm sad," Galarraga said, "but I know that I pitched a perfect game. The first 28-out perfect game."

Eddie the Eagle

The 1988 Olympic Winter Games included some of the greatest athletes in the world. It also included Eddie the Eagle. Eddie was not an actual eagle. He was a ski jumper named Michael Edwards. He had been a downhill skier and speedskater, but he had no real talent at ski jumping.

ANOTHER WILD CARD OLYMPIAN

Twelve years after Eddie the Eagle, another athlete made it to the Olympic Games who wasn't quite elite. Equatorial Guinea swimmer Eric Moussambani was given a wild card spot in the 2000 Games in Sydney, Australia. Only a year earlier, Moussambani didn't know how to swim. He trained himself in a 20-meter pool, while an Olympic pool is 50 meters. As he waited to swim his Olympic heat in the 50-meter freestyle, his other two competitors dove into the water too early. They were disqualified, which meant Moussambani swam alone in front of 17,000 people. As he flailed in the water, the fans cheered him. He finally finished the race with a time of 1 minute, 52.72 seconds, more than a minute slower than the world record.

Eddie the Eagle poses in front of the ski jumps at the 1988 Olympic Winter Games in Calgary, Canada.

HEADS UP!

Sometimes it's an athlete's teammate who deserves most of the blame. During the championship tennis match at the 1912 Olympic Games, Sweden's Sigrid Fick accidentally smashed her partner in the face with her tennis racket. The mixed doubles duo kept playing, but not very well. They lost the gold medal match 6–4, 6–0.

At the time, England didn't have any good ski jumpers. So the country's Olympic committee let Edwards represent England in the Winter Games. Edwards was heavier than the other jumpers and wore thick glasses that fogged up as he jumped. He finished last in both events he attempted. Still, Eddie the Eagle is remembered fondly. At the 2010 Winter Games, Edwards was asked to take a turn running with the Olympic torch.

Bird Problems

The 17th hole at the TPC Sawgrass golf course is famous. The green is surrounded by water. Amateur golfers lose approximately three balls every time they play the hole. Pros don't do much better. Most players, though, don't lose their golf ball when they land it safely on the green.

That's what happened to Steve Lowery at The Players Championship in 1998. When his ball landed on the green, he thought he was safe. But a seagull had other ideas. The seagull nudged Lowery's ball around the green, then picked it up, flew away, and dropped the ball into the water.

Luckily for Lowery, the officials decided the seagull was an "outside agent." They let him put another ball where his original one had landed.

Blame the Band?

On November 20, 1982, the University of California Golden Bears played the University of Stanford Cardinal in a college football game. The two schools are rivals, so the game is a big deal no matter how it ends. Still, this ending was memorable.

With four seconds left, Stanford kicked a field goal to take the lead, 20–19. There was still enough time for one more play.

Stanford kicked off, and that's when things got crazy. The Bears players began tossing the ball from one teammate to another. In total, they tossed it five times. Before one of the tosses, however, the Stanford band mistakenly believed the player had been tackled. So members of the

DRAFT DAY BLUNDERS

Blunders don't have to happen on the playing field. You don't have to look further than the various drafts to see that. The NBA Draft might have had some of the most dubious picks. Future star center Hakeem Olajuwon went first in 1984. Then the Portland Trail Blazers picked center Sam Bowie with the second pick. He went on to play 10 average seasons. Meanwhile, the Chicago Bulls picked Michael Jordan third. He led the Bulls to six NBA titles. The 2003 draft was stacked. LeBron James went first to the Cleveland Cavaliers. Future NBA superstars Carmelo Anthony, Dwyane Wade, and Chris Bosh were available when the Detroit Pistons picked second. Instead they selected center Darko Milicic. He bounced around six teams in 10 seasons and spent most of his career riding the bench.

band marched onto the field. But the game wasn't over.

The California player who had the ball ran around and through the band members to the end zone for a game-winning touchdown. The band didn't necessarily cause the touchdown. But it did make for one of the most memorable plays in college football history.

HOLD THAT BALL!

In 2007, the Dallas Cowboys were one 19-yard field goal away from winning their playoff game against the Seattle Seahawks. Tony Romo, their quarterback and holder, bobbled the snap and couldn't quite scramble into the end zone, and the Cowboys lost.

The *Heidi* Game

On November 17, 1968, the New York Jets played an exciting football game against the Oakland Raiders. The Jets had a 32–29 lead with less than a minute left. Oakland had the ball, though, and the Raiders were driving down the field. Would the Jets be able to stop them? Would they kick a game-tying field goal? Would they score a game-winning touchdown?

Viewers watching the game on TV never got to see what happened next. When the time the network had allotted for the game expired, NBC switched to a TV movie called *Heidi*.

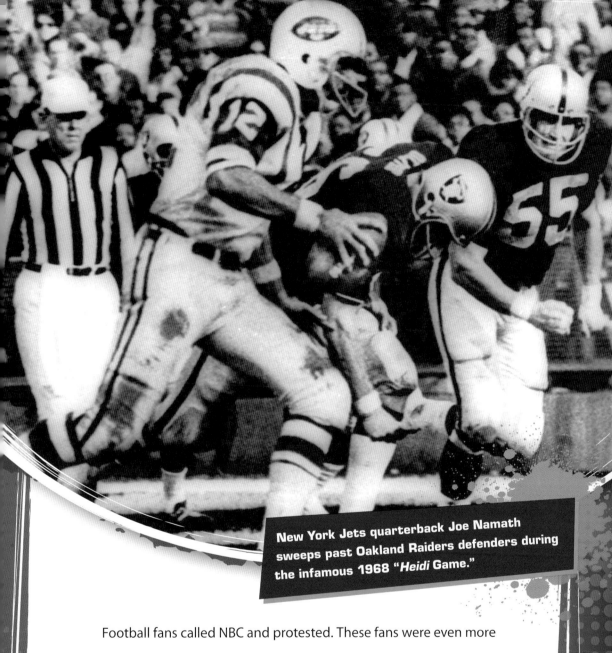

New York Jets quarterback Joe Namath sweeps past Oakland Raiders defenders during the infamous 1968 "*Heidi* Game."

Football fans called NBC and protested. These fans were even more furious when they found out what they had missed. Oakland had scored two touchdowns in less than a minute to win the game 43–32. Their anger was so great that NBC's president, Julian Goodman, publicly apologized.

To this day the game is known as the "*Heidi* Game."

More Bad Scheduling

One afternoon during the 1972 Olympic Games, US sprinter Eddie Hart was watching TV with a couple of teammates. At first, he thought he was watching a replay of earlier Olympic races.

Suddenly, Hart yelled, "Hey! Those are our races!"

He was right. The three teammates made it to the track as fast as they could for the 100-meter dash second round. One of them, Robert Taylor, made it just in time. But Hart and Reynaud Robinson were disqualified. Both had been favorites going into the Games.

What had happened? Apparently, the sprinters' coach had given them the wrong starting times. The coach had been using an old schedule and didn't realize that the schedule had been changed.

Hart and Robinson could only watch as Taylor won the silver medal.

AM I LATE?

Wym Essaja was a runner from Suriname. In 1960 he became the country's first Olympian. On the day of his race, Essaja was given the wrong starting time. He decided to take a nap. By the time he woke up, the race was over.

Not all was lost for Eddie Hart. The sprinter helped Team USA win a relay gold medal in the 1972 Olympics in Munich, West Germany.

That's No Way to End

The 1972 Olympic Games also included a famous basketball blunder. With only seconds left in the gold-medal game, Team USA was losing by a single point to the Soviet Union. US guard Doug Collins stole a pass and raced down the court. As he jumped in the air to shoot a layup, he was fouled. Collins fell to the floor, but finally got up and made his way to the free throw line.

The clock had been stopped with three seconds to go. Collins made the first free throw, tying the game 49–49. He made the second free throw, too. The Soviets quickly inbounded the ball. But the referees blew their whistles to stop the game. They announced that the Soviet coaches had called timeout between Collins' two free throws. Why the officials hadn't stopped the game then wasn't clear.

The referees announced that there were still three seconds left in the game. Again, the ball was inbounded. This time, the final buzzer went off.

Korea's Park Si-Hun, *left*, delivers a left jab to Team USA's Roy Jones Jr. during their 1988 Olympic gold-medal bout in Seoul, South Korea.

The US players thought they'd just won the gold medal. So did their fans. People stormed the court to congratulate the US team.

But then the officials blew their whistles again. They cleared the court. They said that the person running the scoreboard never put three seconds on the clock.

The Soviet Union was given another chance to inbound the ball. This time, the Russian player threw the ball to the other end of the court.

Alexander Belov, the Soviets' star player, jumped up high to snare the ball. He turned and made the layup right before the buzzer sounded.

This time it was the Soviets who did the celebrating. The US players were confused and furious. They felt as though the gold medals had been ripped off their necks. They decided as a team not to accept their silver medals. They also lodged a protest with the International Olympic Committee (IOC). The IOC voted 3–2 in favor of the Soviets.

All these years later, the officials' decisions are still controversial. Whether or not they made the right calls, it's fair to say that they lost control of the game. The US players still haven't accepted their silver medals.

Soviet Union basketball player Alexander Belov scores the winning basket over Team USA in the 1972 Olympic Games.

FUN FACTS

★ Near the end of an NBA game in 2010, the Phoenix Suns trailed the San Antonio Spurs 107–105. The Suns' Jason Richardson, a former slam-dunk champion, stole the ball and dribbled the length of the court, and missed the dunk.

★ Thomas Hamilton-Brown was so sad about losing his 1936 Olympic lightweight boxing match he spent the night eating away his sorrow. It was then announced that there had been a scoring mistake. Hamilton-Brown had won the fight. One problem: the 5 pounds (2.3 kg) he'd gained overnight made him ineligible for the next fight.

★ During a 1986 NHL playoff game, the Edmonton Oilers were tied with the Calgary Flames. That's when Oiler Steve Smith scored a goal—on his own team.

★ Pitcher Tommy John once made three errors—during the same play.

★ At the 1999 British Open, golfer Jean Van de Velde arrived at the 18th hole with a huge lead. He needed only a double bogey or better to win the championship. He made a triple bogey, then lost the tournament in a playoff.

★ In December 1971, the New York Mets traded a young pitcher named Nolan Ryan for six-time all-star Jim Fregosi. Ryan went on to strike out more batters than any pitcher in baseball history. Fregosi hit .233 in 1972.

GLOSSARY

DYNASTIES
Teams that win many championships over a short period of time.

INFAMOUS
Well known in a negative way.

MATCH POINT
In tennis, when a player could win the match with one additional point.

MIXED DOUBLES
In tennis, when a doubles team has one man and one woman.

OBITUARY
A notice of a person's death, often in the form of a short biography in a newspaper.

PLAYOFFS
A series of games or matches to determine a champion.

RIVAL
An opposing team or athlete that brings out particular emotion in a team, an athlete, or fans.

SNOWBOARD CROSS
A competition in which multiple snowboarders start together at the top of a hill and race to the bottom, going over various jumps and navigating other features along the way.

WILD PITCH
A pitch that generally cannot be handled by a catcher and allows a runner to advance.

FOR MORE INFORMATION

Selected Bibliography

"50 Stunning Olympic Moments." *The Guardian*. Guardian News and Media Limited. 25 Jan. 2012. Web. 27 March 2013.

Burke, Monte. "Ten Biggest Blunders in Olympic History." *Forbes.com*. Forbes.com LLC. 29 Jan. 2010. Web. 27 March 2013.

Huebner, Mark. *Sports Bloopers: All-Star Flubs and Fumbles*. Buffalo, New York: Firefly Books, 2003.

Nash, Bruce. *The Football Hall of Shame*. New York: Archway, 1989.

Further Readings

Berman, Len. *And Nobody Got Hurt: The World's Weirdest, Wackiest True Sports Stories*. New York: Little, Brown, and Co., 2005.

Berman, Len. *And Nobody Got Hurt 2: The World's Weirdest, Wackiest and Most Amazing True Sports Stories*. New York: Little, Brown, and Co., 2007.

Berman, Len. *The Greatest Moments in Sports*. Naperville, IL: Sourcebooks, 2009.

Guinness World Records. New York: Scholastic, 2013.

Sports Illustrated Kids Full Count: Top 10 Lists of Everything in Baseball. New York: Time Home Entertainment, 2012.

Web Links

To learn more about the biggest blunders in sports, visit ABDO Publishing Company online at **www.abdopublishing.com**. Web sites about the biggest blunders in sports are featured on our Book Links page. These links are routinely monitored and updated to provide the most current information available.

Places to Visit

Naismith Memorial Basketball Hall of Fame
1000 Hall Fame Ave
Springfield, MA 01105
(413) 781-6500
www.hoophall.com
The Naismith Memorial Basketball Hall of Fame honors basketball's greatest players and moments.

National Baseball Hall of Fame and Museum
25 Main Street
Cooperstown, NY 13326
(888) 425-5633
www.baseballhall.org
This hall of fame and museum highlights the greatest players and moments in the history of baseball.

Pro Football Hall of Fame
2121 George Halas Drive NW
Canton, OH 44708
(330) 456-8207
www.profootballhof.com
This hall of fame and museum highlights the greatest players and moments in the history of the NFL.

INDEX

About the Author

Paul Hoblin has an MFA from the University of Minnesota. He has written several sports books for kids.